Messaging your Business

The Foundation of
Effective Communications

ANN REVELL-PECHAR

For all the precious time and helpful feedback, my thanks to:

Dr. Emily Diamond, Dr. James Revell, Sam Pechar, Tom Pechar, Karen White and my porch sisters,
Mark Johnson, Jerry Coleman, and Cordelia Norris. And thanks for the idea, Nelson Chu.

Balboa Press books may be ordered through booksellers or by contacting:

Balboa Press
A Division of Hay House
1663 Liberty Drive
Bloomington, IN 47403
www.balboapress.com
844-682-1282

ISBN: 979-8-7652-3603-1 (sc)
ISBN: 979-8-7652-3602-4 (e)
Library of Congress Control Number: 2022920515

Print information available on the last page.

Balboa Press rev. date: 12/22/2022

BALBOA.PRESS
A DIVISION OF HAY HOUSE

Messaging your Business

The Foundation of
Effective Communications

About the Youcan DIY Series

Youcan DIY™ is a hands-on workbook series
designed to help small businesses, non-profits, and
startups create and manage their own in-house
subject matter experts. Written by industry leaders
with decades of experience, these short, step-by-step training
books help organizations save money by
managing services that are often outsourced.

These booklets can be paired with custom consulting to assure
keystones are in place and targets are met,
offering a check-in service for additional guidance.
Contact FluentPR for more information.

Contents

How to Use This Book

This book is the first in a series of workbooks and handbooks for small businesses, nonprofits, and startups… in fact, anyone looking to improve their communications/ PR skills. Practically, it is for those who need to communicate about services, products, and overall business but don't have the resources to engage a highly experienced professional to undertake the work.

We encourage you to use and reuse this book. In short, wear it out. You'll probably find it easiest to read it through from beginning to end, and then to go back and complete the exercises once you "get it." Of course, everyone will use the information differently; different tasks will be more important depending on where your organization is in its development. Here's the way we think it's most useful:

1. Take your time

The amount of work that goes into crafting an effective business message will probably surprise you if you don't "live" business communication. Small business owners, entrepreneurs, and people new to these activities can be overwhelmed when trying to do it all at once. So:

Stop after every chapter

Review what we're discussing

Think through your responses

Let it all settle in and then re-read it, noting how the second time through it may come together differently.

2. Think of it as training

This book was developed as more of a workbook than theory or a body of information to be intellectualized. You'll notice there are lots of questions and places to reflect or practice. The concepts don't just sit there as new information to be committed to memory, they encourage action. *Read. Reflect. Then do.*

3. Refresh what you know

Your organization has likely gone through messaging exercises already, maybe with some good results. That's where the "elevator pitch" you use now came from, so you've probably already embraced the goal. But how long has it been since you aligned your organization's key messages with a clear, compelling 2-sentence description? Think of this as your chance to rethink and refine, to retool and keep sharp. Messaging needs to stay fresh.

4. It's a team effort

Participation. Contribution. Buy-in. Founders, directors, and key organizational thought leaders need to be involved. The leadership team will usually identify one communications lead, but they must have a hand in the messaging if the results are to have any chops. While an individual might be responsible for this project, it will take insights from many to achieve solid messaging.

Caution: *with multiple voices involved, there's a risk that your message will get "soupy" and lose its focus and punch. We highly recommend that you keep this exercise to a small group of leaders and influencers in the company.*

5. Get a pencil and notebook

This is a workbook, after all. While we've left places for you to fill in the blanks, some of you will have lots of notes in your margins by the time you're done! Because your first ideas may not be your best or final ones, keeping your thoughts in a notebook may help you work through some of the tasks.

6. Your results and how to use them:

Create a single messaging document *accessible to everyone in your organization, usually in a repository everyone can easily find and use. This will help your colleagues keep your key business message consistent.*

Refer to it regularly. *Mention it in your internal conversations and correspondence, and provide a link or other reminder of where it's kept.*

Purposely use and re-use the words. *Remember, you and your team are the only ones who see the same thing over and over again. Your audience must see your message at least seven times in seven different ways to act on it[1]. So, if you want to get your point across and make it stick, rely on the work you did in this book.*

Revise it *when needed. Always with the buy-in and approval of thought leaders. Subsequently, make sure to socialize the changes.*

Now that you have a handle on what we expect to accomplish together, you probably have had thoughts and reactions, whether organized, thought-through, or not. **Don't lose them!**

Take note:

Take a minute to jot down immediate reactions and takeaways: *maybe people to engage, barriers you'll have to navigate, even a key word or two that you'll want to include in your messaging document.*

ONE

Why Messaging is Mission Critical

The foundation of all communications is messaging. A strong brand also depends on clear messaging. The foundation of all marketing is messaging.

Messaging is important both internally and externally. How so? Knowing and focusing on your key message helps prioritize resources and efforts, and assures consistency in what, how, and to whom you communicate. Keeping your key message front-of-mind makes interviews easier, enables you to communicate more confidently, and helps employees do a better job knowing why they do what they do.

Perhaps most importantly: strong messaging helps customers know the value you can provide to them, because they can trust your organization's own values.

Is a PR message the same as a marketing message?

While they must align and harmonize, a messaging document for use in public relations differs from what a marketing team might assemble. Marketers focus on competitive differentiators, customer benefits, a value proposition, and brand identity. Their objective is to use messaging to zero in on prospects.

PR focuses on mission, vision, and key elements of daily communication, such as an elevator pitch, 50-word descriptions, etc. The difference is that we are not developing ads and sales sheets. We're trying to build trust; we're building a reputation. Trust and reputation cannot be bought—it must be earned. So instead of 'pushing' our product, service or mission, we're pulling people into the fold.

Use messaging to be sure that everyone in your firm is singing from the same hymnal. Use messaging to formulate core values for communication. Use messaging for consistency.

Tips for successful PR messaging:

Viewpoint: *Message from the audience's perspective, not yours. In other words, what is it that the audience needs or wants from you? What benefits (not features) do you offer?*

Clarity: *Use words that your client/customer/influencer will understand. Industry jargon only works within the industry. Keep it there.*

Simplicity: *Start with the very basics of what you do. Explain it simply. Nuance can be added later, but it can interfere with advancement in the early phases of messaging.*

If you're ready to roll up your sleeves, it's time to get started.

A strong and clear message is at the core of all effective organizational communication. It shapes both public opinion and internal culture. Taking the time to dig deeply and find the unique story of your company can bring balance and transparency for the business.

TWO

Who Are You?

Once you're convinced of the need for a clear and compelling statement, the next step is a bit of "organizational navel gazing".

Why? Because successful companies have clear messaging. It requires thinking long and hard about who you are and what makes your organization unique. It takes introspection and analysis to identify the words you will use to create your corporate image or build your brand. Once you know the core of your organization well and have selected words that express it, it's nearly reflexive to pass along to others what is at the front of your mind.

A strong and clear message is at the core of all effective organizational communication. It shapes both public opinion and internal culture. When done well and consistently, it positively impacts organizational success. Yet most young businesses spend little time on their messaging.

It will be hard for an organization to gain market acceptance with a muddy and unclear message. Taking the time to dig deeply and find the unique story of your company can bring balance and transparency to your business.

Corporate Self Awareness: "Know Thyself"

"Know Thyself" was carved into the front of the Oracle at Delphi, and it remains a primary task for individuals as well as the organizations they support.

You can't talk about something you don't know, so let's get down to figuring out who your company is and how to talk about it. In fact, let's think about how individuals are impacted by how well they know themselves.

Research demonstrates that a keen understanding of self can drive both success and satisfaction with life. A *Psychology Today*[2] article (March 2014, *Know Thyself*) said that Oprah Winfrey, regularly on *Forbes* list of self-made billionaire women,[3] clearly understands her 'self' and how that self impacts others.

What do we mean by 'self?' A dictionary definition would say it's a person's essential being, the thing (outside of the body) that distinguishes them from others. It's what makes a person unique. Similarly, a corporate self is the essence of the organization, and what distinguishes it from other businesses and makes it unique.

Over the course of a 30-year career in communications, I've supported the launch of more than 250 products and managed reputations for nearly 200 firms. In that time, I've personally experienced what thought leaders in public relations have known for many years—the company that most clearly communicates its 'self' tends to have the greatest success. To communicate who you are, you must know who you are.

The Society for Corporate and Compliance Ethics referred to the impact that self-awareness has on corporate culture[4]. Companies are made up of individuals, and if you want them to behave as a team, to carry your brand, and to remain strong in face of pandemics and natural disasters, give them the tools to talk about the business effectively. As a new or small business, it's critical that you start early, and understand how to communicate *through* your corporate culture.

Diligently pursue development of your unique and positive corporate culture. We will not undertake that vast topic here but it is an important embodiment of your message: your team represents you everywhere they go.

How do you get to the bottom of who you are as a company? Let's start with what others already think of you.

"…when we see ourselves clearly, we are more confident and more creative. We make sounder decisions, build stronger relationships, and communicate more effectively."

—Tasha Eurich, *Harvard Business Review*[5]

Exercise

Ask three people, at least one of whom is not an employee, to describe your company.

"What do we do?"

Record their answers here (we'll refer back to this as we work on your elevator pitch):

>> *Response 1:*

_____

_____

_____

>> *Response 2:*

_____

_____

_____

>> *Response 3:*

_____

_____

_____

Notes

THREE

The Heart of Your Corporate Self: Mission and Vision

When taking on a new client, one of our first on-boarding tasks is to review the company's current messaging document, if indeed they have one. A messaging document spells out what is important to the company and lays the foundation for all future communication. It should be referred to repeatedly, as it helps hone goals.

Messaging documents come in many shapes and sizes, and different applications and tactics require different messaging. There are four things, however, that startups absolutely must commit to as a viable minimum in a communications-centric messaging document:

> *Mission*
>
> *Vision*
>
> *Elevator pitch*
>
> *50-word description*
>
> *(75- and 100-word versions as well)*

In this chapter we focus on the soul of the company: the mission and the vision, your *raison d'être* or reason for being.

Mission statement

Many people have strong opinions about what a mission statement is and does, but the *Oxford Dictionary* says it is a formal statement of the aims and objectives of the organization.

I say it's what your business will deliver on, every single day.

A good statement helps employees know how to make decisions about their job. It will be shared publicly, so be sure you've been crisp and clear.

Ann's favorite mission statement

The first time I ever heard about a mission statement, I was living in Seattle, where UPS was born. A rumor circulates around there saying that when UPS remade itself to compete with FedEx, a new mission statement was born. That statement is ideal, in my mind:

Get the package there by 10am.

Why? Because everyone in the company can know how to prioritize their tasks. What is it that you, Ms. Employee, will do today to get that package there by 10am?

The mission statement is inspirational. It should allow you and everyone on your team to know how to make decisions. It should inspire your team to excellence. So whether the UPS story is truth or myth, it inspires me.

Create Your Mission Statement

Step 1: Review Your Current Mission Statement

In order to develop the most effective mission statement for your company, start by looking at where you are now. Write your firm's current mission statement here:

_____

_____

_____

_____

_____

_____

_____

_____

_____

_____

_____

Step 2: Colorful Improvement

Take out two different colored pens or pencils. Looking at the two lists below, circle words in your mission statement that fall into the 'include' list with one of the colors, and with the other color circle words/phrases in the 'never include' list.

How does it stack up? Is there more of one color than another?

Include:	Never include:
Goals	Trite/overused words
Actionable words	Jargon
Positive words	Fluff
Reference to your target audience	Vague terminology/ generalizations
What makes you unique	Things that 'everyone' does
Brevity and succinctness	Long, drawn-out platitudes
Your values	Boring me-too-isms

Step 3: Create a mission statement

As you begin your re-write, think not just about what your product or service is, but the impact it has on your customers.

If you could do one thing to make your customers' day better, what would it be?

To get you started, check out this checklist:

- [ ] Get input from the leadership team (they may need a refresher on the definition of a mission statement)
- [ ] Is it memorable?
- [ ] Does it say why you exist?
- [ ] Does it offer a sense of your company's character?
- [ ] Does it incite goodwill?
- [ ] Is it original? In other words, is it differentiated from the competition?

OK, have at it:

Our mission is to…

_____

_____

_____

_____

_____

_____

_____

Step 4: Review and Discuss

Using the checklist, review the success of this draft and make any revisions necessary based on your results. Socialize it with the executive team and get their sign-off.

But before you go carving this in stone, run it by a few other people you trust. Consider other department heads, or board members. Make sure they're giving you honest feedback, and ask:

Could they make decisions about their job based on this mission? Are they inspired by it?

Vision

Entrepreneurs are notorious for focusing on 'now,' citing the length of their task lists. The fact is, if you don't think about why you are in business (above and beyond the making of money), you may not reach the right destination. Just as renowned leadership author Simon Sinek said, "People don't buy what you do, they buy why you do it."

When you're developing your company's vision statement, remember that it is aspirational. *Think long, think hard: in five or 10 years, why is the world a better place because your company exists?*

Here are some questions to inspire you:

Why do you do what you do? Example, Tesla: "to accelerate the world's transition to sustainable energy"

_____

_____

Who will be impacted by your vision? Example, IKEA: "to create a better everyday life for the many people"

_____

_____

_____

What's your corporate passion?
Example, TED Talks: "the power of ideas to change attitudes, lives, and ultimately the world"

_____

_____

_____

_____

_____

_____

What does the world look like when you're successful?
Example, Alzheimer's Association: "a world without Alzheimer's disease"

_____

_____

_____

_____

Now, combine your answers into one impactful statement about how you see the world, because of the work you're doing, being impacted in the next five to 10 years:

_____

_____

_____

_____

_____

_____

_____

_____

_____

_____

_____

_____

_____

SIDEBAR: A Story About Mission vs. Vision

In 1994 I met with Jeff Bezos to pitch our PR and ad agency, explaining why we should launch his startup Amazon. Often touted as Seattle's leading Internet PR firm in those days, we entered with our heads held high. We believed strongly that our keen understanding of "the www" and how it was impacting the world would lead us to victory over traditional firms vying for his business.

But instead he taught me a life lesson. He had a vision for Amazon as it is today, which he kept close to his vest. He kept telling me: Ann, what we have here is the world's first online bookstore, and I need a firm with publishing expertise to promote that.

And I said: Yes, Jeff, but think about this—Amazon can be so much more. You are an internet company, not just a bookstore! You need an internet-focused PR firm.

He shook his head. "But today I am a bookstore. And to become an internet company, I have to succeed here first."

It's been more than 25 years since he said that to me, and so the exact words may be off a little. But the message rang clear. Bezos was someone who understood how to apply his mission and his vision so that he could tune it to the moment and make operational decisions. At that point in the company's development, he wasn't hiring a PR firm to promote the vision. He knew that he would not be in business 25 years later if his 'vision' for an online bookstore wasn't clear and successful.

Today, no one would doubt his vision.

Notes

FOUR

The Elevator Pitch

Book upon book has been written about elevator pitches. You can google to your heart's content and find a wide range of perspectives. Here's mine:

Make it pithy

Make it repeatable

Make the listener want to ask more

So how do you do that? In re-tooling my own business recently, I had a serving of my own dog food. This is not simple stuff, and there's no one right answer.

You've told people about your business ever since the first time you decided to start working on it. You're not new to telling people about what you do. They probably don't know what to do with the information you give them, however. Don't look back at what you have always said; instead, refine your pitch for where you are right now.

Starting the process requires imagination. Literally, imagine you are at a conference and riding an elevator, 10th floor going down. The door opens and the most influential journalist in your industry gets in. There are 3 others there, whom you don't know. You seize the moment and introduce yourself.

"Mr. Mossberg, it's a pleasure to meet you. I'm Ann, and I've started a company that has a completely different approach to PR and communications. Do you mind if I take 30 seconds on this ride to tell you about it?" Assuming there's a smile behind his acceptance, my pitch goes something like this:

FluentPR is addressing the needs of small businesses by helping them grow their own internal communications experts. We start with a custom strategy and PR plan, deliver on consumable content, and support them when it's needed with personal insights. We then create a round-table approach for sharing insights among their peers, overseen by their PR mentor. This saves the company hundreds of thousands of dollars over a two-year period.

Here's what it includes, in just 30 seconds:
- *Company name*
- *Target market*
- *Industry*
- *Unique Selling Proposition (USP)*
- *What's next*
- *Value/ROI*
- *And a lead to get them to ask me a question*

In this case, the question is, "how do you save them so much money?" An ideal opportunity because it speaks to value and the high cost of the traditional PR approach.

Create Your Elevator Pitch

Let's get to it! Revisit what you wrote down from Chapter Two where you noted how others described your company. It may influence what should be included or excluded from your pitch. Take a look at the list on the previous page and start writing. Remember: this is something that is easy to repeat verbally! Keep it simple!

Elevator pitches are difficult. We recommend that, as you review what you've developed, you test it with many people, both inside and outside of your company. Make sure you get the kind of response you're looking for.
If you don't, then revisit it. You may need to do this several times before it's just right.

FIVE

The 50-Word Description

Most companies think this is the easiest part of their messaging, until they try it. Determining the most important thing to communicate is a difficult task. Doing so in 50 words can be excruciating.

You need a 50-word description for all those times your company is being featured somewhere: exhibiting at a trade show, providing a listing for association membership, or applying for an award, just to name a few.

It must be written for a general audience, free of acronyms and hype. Key elements include the official name and headquarters of the company, a mention of key product or service lines, and some element of your unique selling proposition. It is a difficult proposition.

Here is an example:

Fluent PR, a Rhode Island-based communications firm, draws on more than 30 years of expertise in communications, media relations, public speaking, and mentorship. After guiding more than 250 firms and introducing more than 300 tech and biotech products, our new focus on value for small businesses is available at fluentpr.com.

Because we offer so many communications services, I highlighted just a handful to establish expertise and help the reader understand if they are a likely customer. I also chose just one of our three targets, because listing small business, startups and nonprofits gets too heavy. I chose small businesses because startups and nonprofits can relate to a small business, but you may not get a small business owner to relate themselves to a non-profit or startup.

If you're having trouble, start by writing a 100-word description (also often requested by 3rd parties) and then whittle away until you have accomplished the task.

17

The 50-word description must be written for a general audience, free of acronyms and hype. Key elements include the official name and headquarters of the company, a mention of key product or service lines, and some element of your unique selling proposition.

Create Your 50-Word Description

This 'mad-libs' style approach to writing your 50-word description is meant to kick-start your brainstorm. It covers the essentials, but you can play with the order of the items and add more color to your messaging. This will get you started.

_____, a

your company name

_____-based

location

_____,

type of company

_____in order to

what you do

_____. Our key products

why you do it

include _____, and they

product/service name

uniquely _____.

unique selling proposition.

Visit our site for more information, at _____

SIX

Messaging from a Marketing Perspective

Companies focused more on marketing communication (specifically for the purpose of product sales) often include two more pillars in their messaging document: the Value Proposition and the Buyer Persona.

We'll provide a high-level overview here, with pointers on how to get to that ever-elusive perfection. Books and books can and have been written on these two components alone. We're just going to touch the surface, because it will help your messaging in the long run.

The Value Proposition

Value propositions answer the question, why should someone do business with you? To identify your value proposition, begin by writing down five words or phrases that define the tangible value that is unique to your company, or your product/service.

Focus on the benefits you deliver, not features of the products. Let's say that you have developed a new hand-held device, and one of the really cool things about it is that you have included a fingerprint reader. It allows one to login without having to remember their password, and no one else can use the device without your consent.

In this case, don't talk about 'fingerprint login,' because what's important is that we don't have to remember another password. That's why you developed a finger-print login, right?

Step 1: List five different benefits of your product or company that are unique to your business:

1

2

3

4

5

Step 2: Prioritize them. Put the most impactful problem-solving benefits first, and make sure you don't have the 'nice to have' benefit (not feature) at the top!

1

2

3

4

5

Create Your Value Proposition

Step 3: Write a sentence for each of your five benefit statements. For the fingerprint login example above, you might write: "Forget passwords? Sign in with your fingertip."

_____

_____

_____

_____

_____

_____

_____

_____

_____

After playing with at least 5 sentences that represent the value you bring, whittle them down to just two CONCISE sentences that:

Speak to a concern your customers have

Something that you are uniquely able to solve

And explain why what you do is better than what anyone else offers

The key to success of a value proposition? The promise you make to the customer.

We promise to:
Make life easier.
Help you make more money.
Give you three more hours every day.
Let you move on when you forget passwords.

Write your value proposition:

_____

_____

_____

_____

_____

_____

_____

Create Your Buyer Persona

This is where you prove that you really know your customers, and if you don't know them well, this is where you'll get to know them.

Personas are used to create a fictional ideal customer. The information used is taken from data, usually from the research your company has done, about who will most value the products and services your company offers. The data includes demographics, behavior patterns, understanding customer goals, and what motivates them.

If you have a creative bone, this should be fun. It's much like creating a character for a novel. The more specific you make your 'buyer avatar' the more specifically you can market to them, resulting in greater likelihood of the sale and the repeat customer.

Who are your target buyers? Define them in words, and then picture them. Literally.

What are their professions and how long have they been in that role? *Are they newbies or old-hats? Are they professors or vintners? Steel workers or writers?*

What is their role in the organization, or role in the home if you sell directly to consumers? *In other words, are they generally executives? Line workers?*

How will he/she find out about you? *Are they only on social media or are they TV watchers, magazine readers, or tied into a particular social circle that convinces them of your value?*

What pain points does he/she have that you solve?

What does she want, and moret importantly, what does she NOT want?

Bottom line: why will he buy your product?

Personas and avatars are increasingly expected in business. It's a great opportunity to dig in and understand the people who benefit from your solution. Once you undertake this assignment, you will empathize more with your customer and, in turn, do a better job of acquiring and serving them.

You can learn more about buyer personae online—start your search at the American Marketing Association's site (ama.org) as they tend to have regularly updated information. No matter where you search, we highly recommend keeping up with the latest work in this field. Knowing your audience is key to serving your audience.

Notes

SEVEN

The Billboard Exercise

This is a fun way to get to the core of what your pitch might be. It's a tool to help you hone your message, understand what you want people to do with your communication, and keep it tight.

I came up with this idea after a road trip from Georgia to Florida. Interstate 75 is rife with distracting billboards, and during a particularly boring part of the trip I started to get sleepy. A billboard came up that had one graphic element and four words: a coffee cup with the Starbucks logo on the left, followed by "Next exit. Turn right."

They got my business.

What if you could get business that easily? Let's use that example as an exercise.

Imagine that someone, we'll just call that person a 'benefactor', rented billboards across your geographic region. However, due to a change in plans they can't use all of them next month. They've offered your company free use of one of the billboards for a month; you just have to pick the location of the one you want and deliver the artwork.

Of course, you jump on this opportunity for free advertising. But there's the question of the actual billboard, and that task falls squarely on your shoulders.

Two big questions: where and what?

Which location should you choose?

Think long and hard about your customer. What is her day like? Where does he drive on a regular basis?

Once you've considered that, go one layer deeper: when they drive by the sign, are they in a problem-solving mode?

I recently asked this question of a client who is a holistic healthcare provider. She came back to me a week later and determined that she wanted to be near the places where people looking for healthy alternatives will be: near Whole Foods, health food stores, and co-ops. Her thinking was that people who frequent these locations are less likely to need education about why her services are important—they already understand that natural is better. And, because they frequent these stores, they are already thinking about solving a problem when they go there.

So where, physically, is your ideal client? Driving children to school? Regularly on a freeway? Heading into an office park? That's where you want your billboard!

What should it say?

Create Your Billboard

Let's start with the key success checklist:

Seven words or less: when people are driving, and that's generally what they're doing when they see a billboard, they can't digest more than that.

Emotive: make someone care/want to do business with you.

Call to action: don't just push info at them. Pull them into your pitch.

One image: it needs to be clean and easy to read. You can rely on the image to communicate some of what the number of words can't.

Now that you know this, fill in the following to help you decide:

What one message should you communicate?

....

....

....

....

....

....

Who do you most need to reach with this message?

....

....

....

....

Where might those people be most likely to see your sign? (revisit the persona you've developed if you need to think about where they frequent— work, school, church, etc.)

....

....

....

....

What one thing do you want them to do after seeing this?

....

....

....

Draw Your Billboard

You don't have to be an artist, stick figures work fine.

Your Billboard, Option 2

EIGHT

You've Finished: Now What?

You now have the baseline elements of your messaging. You will use these messages throughout your communications—internally, for content creation, and for a broad range of external business communications.

We recommend compiling all the key information into one messaging document. Make sure you have complete sign-off from the executive team and get their agreement to use these messages in the work they do. Circulate the messaging document among all of those on your team that work with the public or your customers.

Your goal is to get everyone who works with your company—employees and partners—"singing from the same hymnal." Don't get bored. Use this messaging over and over again. Remember, potential customers seldom take action until they've seen your message at least six or seven times. If you change the message too often, you may have to start at first impressions all over again.

One of our clients has printed out their final messaging document and keeps it posted above her desk. She found it has had dramatic impact on consistency, and simplified the process for:

Storytelling

Fundraising and annual reports

Product development and competitive analysis

Marketing and sales documents

If you find you want to go deeper, or you're having trouble getting agreement on any of the components, spend time with a communications consultant. By now, you know at least one!

In Conclusion:

Once you've worked through all these messaging exercises, you certainly will 'know yourself' as a company much better. Corporate self-awareness can lead to greater productivity, strong leadership and better communications internally and externally.

Internalizing your company's message forces you to see your company more clearly. This helps you focus, keeps your brand clear, and helps potential customers understand what you can do for them, which ultimately makes the buying decision easier.

You're armed. Go tell your story.

Sources

1 https://www.quora.com/What-is-the-7-times-7-rule-in-marketing

2 https://www.psychologytoday.com/us/articles/201403/know-thyself

3 https://www.forbes.com/self-made-women/#13be6dd46d96

4 http://complianceandethics.org/self-awareness-as-a-foundation-of-a-successful-corporate-culture/ March 2018

5 https://hbr.org/2018/01/what-self-awareness-really-is-and-how-to-cultivate-it

About the Author

Ann Revell-Pechar is the Founder of Fluent PR, Inc., a Rhode Island-based communications firm. Of her 30 years in PR, 25

have been as president of her own firm. She has been instrumental in introducing more than 300 products to market, and managed the messages and reputations of healthcare, technology and venture capital firms worldwide. She's passionate about economic development, startups, travel, and family (which includes her pets).

Printed in the United States
by Baker & Taylor Publisher Services